S,

Thank,
Lemme hear from

you.

D1564984

TALES FROM THE MORGUE

by Michael Ludden

Cover illustration by Charleston, S.C., artist Larry Moore

michaelludden.com
ISBN: 978-1-987599-73-2

Also by Michael Ludden

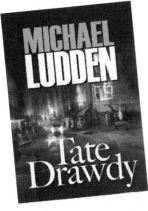

TATE DRAWDY

Amid the engravings of the evangelists, the stained glass, the marble, the serenity of Savannah's Cathedral of St. John the Baptist... two naked bodies. One of the victims is a priest; the other, a teenage girl.

And now John Robert Griffin, a savage killer, wants to help Tate Drawdy solve the crime. That way, there will be more of Drawdy left for him.

Drawdy must survive a horrifying clash with the priest's killer in time to face Griffin. But something's wrong. Drawdy's beginning to suspect someone else out there wants him dead. And he's starting to make mistakes.

A genuine flair for narrative driven storytelling and a master of the mystery genre, exceptionally well written and replete with unexpected twists and turns, "Tate Drawdy" is unreservedly recommended, especially for community library Mystery/Suspense collections.

MIDWEST BOOK REVIEW

Michael Ludden has created a character that likely will make his way to the screen. Up there with the big guys, Michael is a refreshing discovery.

SAN FRANCISCO REVIEW OF BOOKS

I liked Tate Drawdy, the eponymous main character, because he's so, well, normal. His youth and fitness reminded me of

Robert B. Parker's Jesse Stone, but without the unhealthy obsessions. His family wealth reminded me of W.E.B. Griffin's Badge of Honor series set in Philadelphia, but Tate doesn't have a chip on his shoulder. Unlike so many police characters, Tate isn't a drunk, an addict, a hound dog with women, or morosely past his prime. Instead, Tate is a smart, savvy, resilient, and... his sense of duty provides often thrilling edge-of-your-seat moments in the book.

CARMEN AMATO, AUTHOR OF THE EMILIA CRUZ NOVELS

"A rollicking tale with plenty of gunplay, suspense, ribald banter and plot twists that brings you to the final chapter way too soon... "

JIM NESBITT, AUTHOR OF THE ED EARL BURCH NOVELS

Michael Ludden's second foray into the crime fiction world currently dominated by authors such as Michael Connelly, James Ellroy, and Harlan Coben, is as satisfying as his first ("Alfredo's Luck"), but is enhanced by a more sharply-drawn protagonist, and believably-evil miscreants... Ludden's convincing cast, supple plot, and tight action comprise a highly satisfying read. And the aforementioned gimlet-eyed descriptions of facial features; the streets, buildings, flora, and humidity of Savannah; and even how long it might take someone to dust an intricate chandelier will make you grin at the cleverness of it all.

POSTED ON AMAZON

I can always measure a book but how much I do not want to put it down. If I get to beddy-bye time and say "egh, 15 more minutes reading", then I know that I like the book. Mr Ludden passes that test big time. He has cost me sleep, lots.

POSTED ON AMAZON

I can't recall the last time I enjoyed a work of detective fiction as much as I've enjoyed this title. Mr. Ludden is very, very smart and an extremely good writer. He's paid his dues in another career and didn't write his first work of art during in-school detention in elementary school. Because of this—I may mistakenly believe—he doesn't feel the need of so many other mystery/thriller writers to literally fill-in all the blanks, answer all the questions of mankind, and dump a bunch of happy, sappy endings in the last eight pages of his book.

Beyond that compelling plot and the delight of working to stay ahead of the writing by solving these mysteries on your own is the author's ability to set the scenes with such wonderful detail. He puts you in the scene, so much so that you can feel the tension, see the rooms, the crooked, broken walkways, the gracious old homes and then share the fear of knowing that gunshots, a knife or a brutal assault lurk at the edge.

A great Southern Crime Thriller that goes through a lot of beers, bandages and bad guys. Who did it is never too much in doubt, but how and why they did it will keep you turning the pages. I really enjoyed the ride

(Ludden's) writing is elegant and visceral at once. Fortunately for us there are more Tate Drawdy books on the way. Michael Ludden has created a character that likely will make his way to the screen. Up there with the big guys, (Ludden) is a refreshing discovery.

The man knows psychology, food, clothing, architecture, cars, police workings, libations, and so much more, and (Ludden) discloses his knowledge in fascinating and minute detail! I love books built around good relationships and clever solutions to daunting dilemmas, and (he) does not disappoint on either count.

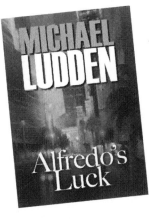

ALFREDO'S LUCK

Miami detective Tate Drawdy's girlfriend won't marry him. His boss can't stand him. And the hottest Cuban in the city has just been murdered on his watch.

Drawdy's about to discover the victim was the wrong man. A case of mistaken identity? He's going to find out. But first, a terrifying encounter with an escaped con. And, ain't this a thrill? He's beginning to suspect the guy he's trying to protect is running some sort of expat conspiracy.

Drawdy's a rich kid who dropped out of med school to become a cop. He's impetuous. He's a blues fanatic — bring your earplugs. And his obsession with this case is about to get him killed.

A well written tale of honor, loyalty, impossible dreams and ultimate betrayal. Riveting, fast-paced story with characters you'll love and characters you'll hate. Buckle up and enjoy the ride...

Fast paced with plenty of twists and turns. Loved it!...

A page-turner that keeps the mind working with twists and turns and enough drama and complex characters to challenge the best of the crime genre...

The suspense grabs you with layers of possibilities. The perps, the victims and the cops are proliferating like weeds. You won't solve it, most likely, but keep your eye on Tate as he puts investigative instinct to work while risking his all...

I found Alfredo's Luck captivating from the very first page. As each chapter finished I was compelled to begin the next; until before I knew it—it was over. And I was like, "Whew, what a ride! Let's go again...

Fantastic twists and turns kept me turning the pages. The author clearly knows his territory and subject. The descriptions were vivid, the characters well-developed and varied, the plot engaging. Put it at the top of your summer reading list!...

Michael Ludden's recent contribution to the crime/detective genre is an undiluted pleasure. The pacing is fast, the language spare and the action taut...

Check out our website at
www.michaelludden.com

Tales from the morgue

MICHAEL LUDDEN

This book

I don't think I knew I wanted to work for a newspaper until I did. But it tends to grow on you.

The best thing was all the crazy, different stuff you got to do every day. Great stories. And great stories behind them, too. Some uplifting. Some tragic.

Like the time I found myself trapped in a barn (surrounded by elephants); getting close enough to feel the pounding on your chest as the shuttle roared into space; climbing into a cage with a mountain lion; sifting through the remains of a jetliner after it smashed through a neighborhood; being on the wrong side of a dictator's rage.

I'd gotten my first job not long after I got out of school. It was a weekly, The Hilton Head News, a bureau of the Savannah Morning News. I asked the editor for some freelance work. No money, he said. I offered to work for free. (Hey, it was the beach.)

He let me write a couple of stories, then offered me a job. The kicker was when he asked if I was proficient in the darkroom. I lied and said yes, then got a guy to teach me.

I think I had 12 or 13 beats and let's just say I was horrible. And so confident, I wrote everything out longhand on a legal pad before I typed it up. (Glacier speed.) The editor used to stand in front of my desk screaming. Sometimes he jumped up and down. That was good training. And once a week, I got a check for about what you would spend on a nice steak today.

It was the first of a bunch of great jobs where the people I worked for didn't mind if you wrapped some of the drama into your reporting, if you talked about what things looked like... what they smelled like... how it felt... Maybe if we'd had more of that kind of writing... well that's another story.

Soon, I was offered a job at the local daily, an afternoon paper, The Beaufort Gazette. We started at 6 and had to go out and get stories and write them by 11. Three or four a day. That's when I learned to write (very) quickly and where I began drinking 10 cups of coffee every morning and smoking a pack a day.

Both those papers were tiny, compared with The Orlando Sentinel, where I went two years later and where I spent the next 20 years. Florida was the nation's newspaper battleground in those days and Orlando was fat. Tons of money, tons of talent, lots of staff, big ambition. Fabulous place to work.

And for quite a while there, I got to cover pretty much whatever I wanted. Bad guys, politics, refugees and many of the kinds of head-shaking stories we've come to associate with Florida. It's where I learned to love it. And where I started thinking... 'wow. I don't have to work for a living.'

The stories in this book are pretty close to what ran in the paper, although I stuck a bit more of me in there than would have been appropriate in the straight-news days.

And they're true.

A lot of the people who read my blog harangued me to put this book together. Even my wife thought it was a good idea, but only if I stuck in a picture of the cat. So, here you go...

...Little

Contents

Ringside with Ali's sparring partner…

I think this whole mixed martial arts thing came out of the old Tough Guy Fights. That's when promoters figured out guys would show up in droves to see amateurs try to destroy each other.

I showed up for one of the early ones. Staggered fights, based on weight. The lightweights first. The heavies at the end.

I get there early. They're just putting up the ring. Out comes Solomon McTier. Guy's in his 50's, owns a bar a few miles down the road. What you need to know is Solomon was a Golden Gloves champ… here and abroad. And the fact that he was the sparring partner for many years for Muhammad Ali.

I'm hanging out ringside when Solomon walks in, asks one of the guys: "Is this so and so's old ring?"

It is.

"I remember it had a soft spot," he says.

And he spends the next 10 minutes tiptoeing around, lightly bouncing on the mat, moving his feet a few inches at a time. Until he finds it.

The fights begin. Some drunk from the audience stands up, says he can fight. They put him in the ring. Somebody else gets in with him. Kicks his ass.

It goes like that.

Then the main event. Solomon walks out in a silk robe. And out steps a grinning tyrannosaurus who looks like he could pick up your car with one hand. His arms are bigger than my thighs. 24 fights. 24 victories. 22 by KO. All those fights, by the way, took place behind the walls at Florida State Prison, his home for the last 10 years after the misunderstanding that ended up with a guy getting killed.

He's about 25. When they meet center-ring, Prison boy is real tempted to laugh at Solomon, who now sports a good-sized gut and gray hair.

Prison's gonna make quick work of grandpa.

They begin to circle each other, throwing jabs, sizing each other. Solomon can toss a fist out and have it back in front of his chin in about the time it takes for you to blink.

But prison boy can dance. And he can throw a punch that is so scary you think it would turn anything it hits into kindling. A few clinches. Mostly Solomon's keeping his distance. He looks a little worried. Prison's got a big smile.

I'm sitting right outside the ropes. And I've memorized the spot, still wondering what it means.

A couple of rounds in. All of a sudden, Prison lands a huge shot on top of Solomon's chest, right at the shoulder. Solomon's arm falls. It's hanging, dragging down by his ribs. He's trying to hold it up and retreating across the ring.

Prison thinks it's a ruse and waves at Solomon to get back on the horse. But Solomon's hunched over and Prison is not the most patient guy. He closes in and starts knocking the crap out of him. Solomon's bobbing, weaving, taking most of the hits on his arms, leaning back into the ropes. He's dodging the worst of it, but you know it's just a matter of time until one of those haymakers sends him into next week.

Solomon's shuffling across the ring. And guess what? He's getting real close to that spot.

Now he musters one last charge. He goes after Prison. But then he takes another shot. Seems like a glancing blow, but it rocks him back. Prison closes in. Solomon's leaning heavily into the ropes.

He's timing it.

As Prison lunges, Solomon throws himself backward, bouncing off the rope just as Prison sinks into that soft spot. Solomon is moving, hard, fast, the right arcing over Prison's head.

Boom. Cocky don't live here no more.

Prison is airborne. He floats back, suspended, a look on his face that says he has just lost any recollection of life on this planet.

Lands with a thud. Big thud. After several minutes, they give up trying to get the boy to make any sense. They cart him off like a fat child still learning to walk.

Folks want Solomon to hang out, take some bows.

Nah. Gotta go. Nice seeing ya.

The streets are paved with gold...

E verybody knew the Cubans could play ball. Seemed like so many guys there, born with gloves in their hands.

There was a period, back in 1980, during the Mariel Boatlift, when the city of Miami started putting tons of Cuban refugees under the old Orange Bowl. When I say under, I mean on the ground, under the bleachers. Cots, blankets, big piles of empty wine bottles.

Over their heads, lush turf, glistening paint, a scoreboard like something they'd only seen on television, lots of places to buy food, when a game was on. But these folks couldn't go up there, not even to look.

Eight long weeks in the heat. The government brought em stuff to eat and drink. People sneaked in some booze. Nobody was gonna grumble.

So they sat. They smoked.

One day a city guy shows up with a bat and ball, a couple of old gloves. Guys grab em and sprint out to the lawn outside the stadium. Old guys and kids and wives and girlfriends follow to sit and watch.

The guys toss their shirts. And what they know right now is that they have just a few minutes. Then the buses will arrive to take em miles from here, out to the middle of nowhere to a tent city where the controversy over whether these people are going to be allowed to stay in the United States is going to be just that much more muted. Further out of sight.

They'll stay there, behind fences.

So they race onto the field, begin to throw it around. But this is not casual pitch and catch. We're talking 50 yards apart, snapping off gorgeous throws, long and hard, that crack into the glove. They move like cats.

A guy picks up the bat, walks over to a bald spot. Pitcher cranks one at him, whistles it down the middle. Boom. Guy out in center sprints back... back... leaps, stretching for it. He pulls it in, spins, fires it home. And that ball is comin.

The people cheer.

And then it ignited...

O ne of the great perks of Florida journalism was covering the space program during the heydays. Back in the day, people used to line up along the beach in Cocoa to see a launch.

And when it was time for the first shuttle to go up, a million people crammed in, shoulder to shoulder. Got there early.

That was as close as the public could get, but it was miles away.

If you had the right creds, you could get to the press site, 3.5 miles across Mosquito Lagoon from the launch pad. Now, if 3.5 miles sounds like a long way to be from a rocket launch, you've never been that close.

Let's just say whatever you see on television is a ridiculous imitation of the blinding light, the roar, the thunderclap-pounding, chest-bruising barrage that is about to wash over you like a tidal wave. The folks who wanna stand lean into it.

The first launch had been a ticking clock for years. Delays... safety concerns... debate... fixes.

Money.

More delays. Like a lot of folks, we went and came home, went and came home, camped out in the parking lot with buckets of fried chicken and large quantities of unauthorized sustenance. Always waiting for Go.

Generally, the countdown's gonna run down to mebbe nine minutes and some change, even on a bad day. It's when you start

getting into those final-minute checks that you're most likely to
see red lights start to blink.

Well on April 12, 1981, the lights stayed green. The clock kept
ticking. And in the concrete bleachers, under that galvanized
roof, a sea of reporters and tv guys from all over Florida and
the U.S. and the world started to get out of their seats, started
walking, quickly, down toward the water.

Stopped talking.

And then it ignited. Main engines hammering so hard you
could see the frickin engine nozzles shaking like they were about
to fall off and even the damn tail was shaking. (Something else
to fix later.) And then it started to lift off the ground.

Slowly at first, as if it were too big, too heavy to compete with
gravity. And then unimaginable acceleration... glorious, stunning, violent. The flames underneath, so brilliant it was painful
to watch. And yet it danced into the heavens as if it weighed
nothing at all. Disappearing all too quickly.

Look around at all the hard-case journos. Screaming, tears
flooding down their faces, sobbing, arms raised, hands clasped.
Somebody's hanging on to a railing. And then the shouts.

"Oh my God!"

"God bless America."

"Brezhnev... kiss my ass!"

You wanna take the stick?

I'm getting what they call an orientation flight. With the Blue Angels. Public relations.

Who cares? I would cut off my arm to get in this thing.

Friend of mine drives me out to the airport, a smallish place south of town where they can do stunts and not be in anybody's way. She's gonna watch. From the ground.

Safety lecture first... parachutes, etc.

I sit in the back. We're getting ready to hammer it and he says... "What I like to do to start is called a performance climb. I'm gonna lift the wheels off the runway, put the jet on its tail and hit the burners. We'll go straight up, very fast. Are you cool with that?"

Are you kidding?

We do the climb, we run around up there, sitting atop a jet engine that can knock down a house, destroying the clouds. He catapults, stunts. And I dunno if the jet jockeys do this for everybody to make em feel special, but at one point he says, "I'm gonna put it into a high-G turn. We'll see how you tolerate it. If it's too much, call out on your mic."

I watch the meter roll up to about 6 and half Gs. I'm flexing my stomach hard, to keep it where it's supposed to be. You do not see this flying Delta, but in turbulence, these wings rock like whitecaps in the wind.

"How was that?" he says.

Do not stop on my account, I say.

At which point, he says... "It seems like you're real good with it. I was supposed to practice today and ran out of time. If you don't mind and you got no place to go, we could run through the show. Take about a half hour."

I was figuring my flight would be 10 minutes, at best. I tell him it sounds something along the lines of spectacular.

We are booming a pirouette into the sky when he says... "You wanna take the stick?"

Three guesses, pal.

So I get to climb and dive and spin and bash my frickin head against the sides of the cockpit from pushing the thing too hard. We go into a steep climb and he tells me to level it off, at which point we go weightless.

"You need to be a little more sensitive with the stick," he says.

"I am available for more practice," I say.

I am flying with a guy who spots a smokestack miles in the distance, says we're gonna stick our nose in it (after a few intermediate steps). Proceeds to hammer inside loops, outside loops... a whole lot of stuff where I cannot see the ground and, in fact, have no idea where it might be at that particular moment.

We are screaming out of a high speed turn when I see our nose is now pointed straight down, dead center on that smokestack.

Finally, we gotta quit.

I am trying to find some way to thank the guy.

Can I buy you a house?

We float lightly onto the runway, climb out. My friend and chauffeur runs outside, wants to know if I threw up.

Hell no. Are you kidding? That was the best thing I've ever done in my *life*.

Wish I could say the same, she says.

But that thing you did, going straight up off the runway. That was bad.

Interview with a dictator...

So I'm heading down to Haiti to interview Baby Doc Duvalier, dictator son of a dictator. He's been interviewed before, but this is 1980 and tons of Haitians are piling onto anything that floats these days and heading for Florida, so I'm not alone. Mebbe three other writers and a photographer show up. It will be the Doc's first 'group' session.

We're escorted way outa town to a mansion overlooking the harbor at Port au Prince. Hollywood has nothing on this place. It is staggering. Marble, crystal, lush woods. Lot of money.

Along the perimeter, there's a guy with an Uzi every 20 feet. Sounds like an exaggeration. Take my word. There are a ton of guys standing guard here.

I ask the ranking guy around, who turns out to be the Finance Minister, if this is where the Prez lives. I've seen the palace downtown, which looks like a French chateau and runs for blocks, separated by a fence and another army of guards from the starving islanders who beg for handouts across the street.

He laughs at me, says it is for weekend entertaining of "very unimportant guests." About this time we hear the Doc heading up the winding one-lane that climbs the mountain to this little shack. I've just been up this road, moving at about 5 mph to snake through the throng of people and tiny homemade carts lugging firewood.

The reason we can hear Duvalier's on his way: Sirens, dozens of motorcycle cops and the fact that he's got his big Benz screaming. As for all those poor people crammed onto that little road, they can jump out of the way or they can be dead poor people.

Duvalier arrives. Before he steps out of the car, it is surrounded by machine-gun toting guys standing shoulder to shoulder. The Doc runs this place with fear and murder and torture. He is never exposed.

We go inside. Begin to talk. There's a delay as his guy translates in both directions. It is obvious from second one that Duvalier has nothing to contribute, is an inarticulate slob and has so much disdain for this moment that it's oozing out his pores. His three-word responses turn into paragraphs of lofty prose in the hands of his translator.

And it is during one of these moments, amid the palms and the cool island breezes and the chandeliers, as the dictator continues to spout, that one of the uncouth American swine journalists gathered there on his marble porch decides to interrupt with another question.

It happens so quickly it takes a moment to fully register. The guard standing just behind His Eminence has whipped that little Uzi waist high. He's either about to cut loose or he's doing a real good job of intimidation.

The clue might be the fact that my new best friend, the Finance Minister, has grabbed the barrel and yanked it to the floor.

Nobody interrupts Baby Doc.

A few hurried comments later, the interview is over. There are no refreshments.

Are you some kind of witch doctor?

I 'm sitting with the old sheriff, his big desk between us. He's cheerful, smiling, telling stories... back in the day.

Behind him and along the walls, rustic paintings, shields, masks. On the desk behind me, a collection of dolls, stuff for potions.

This is his office.

He downplays his reputation, but as we're talking, there's a spark, a flash of light.

Something just flew through the air. A tiny bolt of lightning? A visitor will flinch when something unseen collides in the corner of a room.

He smiles. He's amused, keeps talking.

Ed McTeer was a South Carolina sheriff when Beaufort County was still a patchwork of islands populated by shrimpers and netmakers, basket weavers and root doctors.

McTeer, something of a medicine man himself.

Hard to imagine people today could enforce law and order as he did then. He'd drive out some sandy road, pull over to chat with some folks. If you see Aaron, he'd say, tell him I'd like him to come in.

And he would. Even if it meant jail.

Fair amount of respect.

A tall man, thin, comfortable with his life. They built a new bridge out to Lady's Island and named it after him.

His daddy had been sheriff. Ed grew up around former slaves and learned the ways. And he learned it's what people believe that matters.

When his father died, Ed took over his job. He was 22, mebbe 23, still a kid, really. Those were Model-T days, back in the late 20s.

And for nearly 40 years, McTeer would run things. A lifetime. As the years passed, the legend grew. The man had a power. It was best to comply. Others might use that power for darkness. Not Ed.

He would say it was just a matter of understanding people, getting to know them.

He could have felt alone. This was a place said to be full of haunts. But the thing about Ed, he was confident. He learned some conjuring from the old men, he said. And he was born with a gift.

He tells more stories, but it's all about the same thing. His kind of lawman was gentle, easy, respectful. But he was tough. He didn't step away from a challenge. He kept the peace. Didn't carry a gun.

But he could cast a spell.

I walk to the door. There's a sudden crackling and I can smell smoke. I look, but there's nothing there.

We try to skip a bar tab… and go down in flames…

Many years ago, there was an old bar across the street from our newspaper office. Grungy place. Cheap beer, greasy burgers, jukebox. Tables so wobbly you'd have to put a brick under one leg.

Place was fabulous.

One night, bunch of us are over there telling war stories. The clock winds. Finally, there's nobody left but me and another guy. Alex Beasley… good storyteller.

We figure our boss is still working late. So we get the bartender to call the newsroom, ask for Jim Toner.

He dials the phone.

Is this Toner? he says. Coupla guys were in here. Drank up half the place. Then they left, said to call you for the tab.

Hangs up. Turns back to us.

It's not gonna fly, guys.

Why? What did he say?

He said: "Tell Ludden and Beasley it won't work."

Looking for a ride into space...

I'd been covering prison breaks and politics and refugees and killers and dopers. And then lately I'd done some work on the space program.

Science stuff, explanatory stuff. What makes the shuttle go. The cooling system that keeps the auxiliary power boosters from overheating tends to ice up. So it's got a heater. But that gets too hot, so it's got a cooling system. And so on.

One day I get a call from a long-time space writer. Wants me to know NASA has just published a book of what it thinks is some of the best writing about the program.

Some of your stuff is in there, he says.

Well I think that's pretty cool and we talk awhile about the book and how NASA has a portion of its funding devoted to education, how it may be the only federal agency that takes the public relations job truly to heart.

Great people, the folks at NASA.

In the midst of this chat, he mentions there's going to be a seat on a shuttle set aside for a journalist. He's telling me about it. (This is the same program that will soon put schoolteacher Christa McAuliffe on board the Challenger, the ship that blew up just after launch on Jan. 28, 1986.) First, a teacher, then a journalist.

I interrupt.

Call em, I said.

There's no thinking about it in my case. I'm there. Right now.

I go on to say I run about 20 miles a week, play tennis, don't smoke, eat the occasional salad. Be happy to take a leave of absence. The truth is, I would give just about anything to fly into space

Do me a favor. Call em.

Now it's his turn to interrupt. And he tries, but I keep talking. If they need me to do some kinda program, be happy to do it. I've already done some stunts in a Blue Angels fighter and that thing pulls a bunch more Gs than a measly shuttle. I'll shave the beard.

Settle down, he says. There's a sign-up thing.

Not interested, I say. Call whoever it is and tell em I will sign whatever they need.

The word is already out on this, he says.

I can hear it coming. So... somebody got there ahead of me?

Thousands of people, he says.

Terrific.

Surrounded by elephants...

I'm heading out to find a circus taking a break. It's winter time. The Clyde Beatty show is hunkered down out in the middle of nowhere, waiting for spring. I drive a couple hours, find the place. There are lots of old buildings and sheds and clusters of cages stacked high, some old railroad cars. You can hear lions roaring, which is pretty cool. But there aren't any people. None.

I start hiking across this field. Way in the back there's a big barn. Still nobody. I get to the barn. Knock. Nothing. I go in. From bright sunlight into total darkness. It's gonna take days for my eyes to adjust.

I start shuffling slowly into the room, then stop, realizing I can't see my hand in front of my face. Just the slightest sense of creepy. Probably a better idea just to wait a minute.

So I stand there. Not sure if it's my imagination, but I think I can hear something. A faint... touching. Mebbe it's a mouse tiptoeing across a bed of hay. I'm concentrating now, hard. Another touch off to my left. I wait. I still can't see.

Another, but I'm not sure. But now there's something else. A sense. I feel something—in the air around me. Take my hands outa my pockets. I'm just beginning to be able to see. I'm in a room, a smaller room than I expected, with high walls. There's that sound again. Now it's coming into focus, the wall. And it seems to be coming closer. It's more of a circle. It's becoming a circle.

Elephants. A bunch of em. Every one of em, staring.

I walked into their barn. They surrounded me and I barely heard squat. They're stepping feather-light. How do they do that?

Closer now.

At the same moment, this is perhaps one of the coolest things I've ever experienced and mebbe not so cool. You start wondering if the small human has done anything that might aggravate the pachys. It's not like I had permission.

I can see the door behind one guy. I walk up to him.

Up to his thigh.

I give it a slap. Not a hard slap. Not a stupid slap. But a firmish, confident slap, the kind you use when you move elephants aside on a regular basis. Coming through, I say.

Big Boy ain't movin.

I'm committed. So I squeeze. It is not easy. He stands firm. I get skinny.

Shut the door behind me.

The jet went down in a residential neighborhood...

I t was Kenner, Louisiana, outside New Orleans. July 9, 1982. At the time, it was the second worst air disaster in U.S. history. All 145 on board died, along with 8 killed on the ground.

You could never walk around the wreckage these days. Somebody would have roped it off. Back then, it was just a matter of following the smoke.

Pan American Flight 759 dug a trench three football fields long when it came down. Some said it flew too low and hit a tree. Later, they decided it was wind shear.

Sudden fire. The jet spewed blazing fuel all along its path. It smashed everything to bits. In the branches of trees above the smoking fuselage, you could see tattered pieces of clothing. Just short of where the jet came to rest was another tree. High up in a crook was a stuffed bear. At first, I thought I'd spotted the body of a child.

Early on, it was just rescuers, cops and firefighters and airport safety crews. They showed up with bags of ice and gloves and body bags and masks.

Mute, staring. Doing everything they could. At first they hurried. But then it sank in. This would take days, weeks. They gathered up scorched shoes, tires, twisted bits of metal, parts of suitcases, anything that looked like it could have been human.

Dignity, gone. Families, gone.

Impossible angles, trees snapped off, blasted into kindling, a burnt-out car, a slab without a house on it, the slab split in two. A refrigerator.

I was there all day, and all day long I heard people scream, "there's a child in that tree!"

This was the neighborhood so close to the runway a little kid got famous one day.

He threw a tennis ball in his back yard. Threw it up into the air and hit a plane.

You are now leaving the United States...

I'm heading out to the Yoruba Nation. This place is off a rural two-lane south of Yemassee, South Carolina, where you pass a sign telling you when you've left the confines of the U.S.

This is still the U.S., to be truthful about it. But you are in the middle of nowhere.

Some law enforcement types are real interested in this place. They think it's a hideout for a bunch of guys robbing banks up and down the east coast, collecting food stamps on their off days. I don't know about that, but I can tell you, I only see a couple of women in the whole place, very young. Everybody else is male and ripped.

Could be just the time of day.

It's basically a camp in the woods at the end of a dirt road. Some buildings made out of plywood, under the trees. Metal roofs. Not much to it. Music playing on a loudspeaker someplace. You can pay a few bucks to see the place. Or you can say you're a newspaperman looking for the head guy.

I get directed to a small building where we sit on some mats. It's a dirt floor. One of his wives brings us some water in a jelly jar. Colorful rugs and African art on the walls. A broom made of straw.

Charming guy, funny, articulate. He's actually from up north, but he spent some time in Nigeria and started this place to be about religion, getting back to your roots, disavowing material- ism, being authentic, connected with the ancient culture.

They live pretty simply out here, drive into town once a week for necessities. We talk awhile about what people believe, how they choose to live, what's important to them.

This place is still getting its start. In a few years, there will be more people. The tourists will come to see dancing and sculpture and festivals.

Right now, it's in the 90s and we're sitting on the ground. The air is not moving. I swat at some flies.

He smiles, cocks his head. We push open a little door, duck through an opening.

Aahh.

Much bigger room. You can stand up in here. Air conditioning. Stereo, big TV. Stretch out the kinks, drop into a nice, soft chair.

"You want a beer?"

You can get in the cage with the lion if you want…

Guy on the coast has his own little zoo. Some big cats. 40 acres, some bears, some monkeys, some birds.

Now he wants to sell the place. That's gotta be tricky. I drive out with a photographer named Dennis Wall, who has kind of a wry sense of humor.

We talk to the guy awhile, walk around. Dennis gets a buncho pictures, glamour shots of the animals. We're walking by one of the cages. It's a mountain lion. Guy says the lion is super tame, a really nice lion.

"You can get in there with him if you want."

We laugh.

"No kidding. People do. You sit down, he'll come over and rest his head in your lap. You can scratch him."

Who said my momma didn't raise no fools?

I open the cage.

Dennis has his camera up. That's after he tells me I'm a frickin idiot.

I climb inside. Sit in the back, lean against the wall. Lion saunters over. (Lions don't walk, am I right? They pad. They slink. They *move noiselessly*.) Saunter is ok in this case.

He saunters over, puts his head in my lap. Proceeds to purr, which is very cool, because his purr is way more satisfying than the kind of purr you associate with, say, a house cat.

It's more of a rumble. From a truck.

I scratch behind his ears. At this point, we are brothers. And I wanna hang out.

Dennis gets a couple cool pictures. Gives me one.

I send it to my mom, just to dispel any doubts.

Going to jail for what!?...

M iami to Haiti on Air France. We have just touched down on the runway.

All the sudden, the jet lurches violently sideways. Brakes screaming. People screaming. I look out the window. Here's an old fart pedaling a bicycle, right down the center line of the runway.

He's not looking at us. Guess he figures it's his country. Bike's as old as he is. He's got two hens tied to the handlebars, two more tied over a little rack behind his seat.

We pull up to the gate. Actually it's a doorway.

Tons of people inside. The big difference between this and, say, an American airport... I can't really spot any booths, desks, gates, officials, places where you're supposed to stand, signs.

There are a bunch of guys walking around carrying Uzis, though. This is 1980 and Baby Doc Duvalier is still in power. We won't see airports this gunned up for another 20 years.

I've booked a car. Now I'm not real sure who to ask. I go up to a guy. Machine gun, sidearm, boots, puffy pants. All he's missing is the bandolier.

Rental cars? I ask.

No answer.

I keep looking. Finally a guy with a little notepad comes up, asks if I'm the guy who wanted the car.

Do I stand out in this crowd?

Minute later, I am waiting outside, bag over my shoulder, as this guy drives up in a VW that might have something like 300,000 miles on it. No way to tell. None of the stuff on the dashboard works. It's leaning to one side, lotta rust. Not sure who's been sleeping in here.

Hands me the keys.

I hop in, head downtown. One thing you figure out real quick when you're driving in Port au Prince. Other drivers do whatever they frickin please. And the whole thing about watching out that you don't hit somebody...? Ain't no big thing.

Same with the people. They wanna step in front of you. Might be the most interesting thing that happened to em all day.

At least the window works. It's 100 degrees. No breeze.

Houses made out of scrap lumber, roofing material, chunks of billboard. Amid all the poverty, incredible artwork. The houses, the cars, everything is painted.

I get to the hotel. Holiday Inn. Go to the bar. Nice wood, somber lighting, smooth jazz. Americans are tucked in here. I start talking with a guy who turns out to be a long timer in these parts.

How was the flight, he asks. I tell him about the cyclist on the runway with the birds, how that was nothing compared to the crazy drive into town.

You rented a car?

At this, he is stunned. He points out he would never rent a car in this country for any reason.

Never.

I don't wanna go to jail, he says, for running over a chicken.

This teacher is going to tell the truth, the whole truth....

W e want to look at how teaching school these days is like pushing that big rock uphill. We do a bunch of stuff in the classroom. With kids.

The piece de resistance is gonna be a diary. An anonymous diary, from a teacher telling it like it is. We spend a lotta time finding someone who's mature, but idealistic. Young, but savvy.

Take her to lunch. She talks for hours about the frustrations. Every question sparks a litany.

All the kids do is memorization. The course work is relentless, stupid. They get to bring their notes to exams. Day after day, they won't pay attention. They don't care. They get drunk. They get stoned. They have sex in the bathroom.

They fight. She's not allowed to do anything about it.

Nothing.

For most of the tests, they get a copy in advance. (They get a copy in advance.) Half of em, still flunking. Bottom line, she is *not supposed* to flunk these kids and they are flunking in droves.

Don't ask what happens when she tries to visit with mom and pop.

The lunch crowd has shrunk down to us. Nobody else. Except the waiter, who has stood just off to the side for the last two and a half hours while we talked.

Finally, the guy comes over.

I hate to do this, he says. I never eavesdrop. I never interrupt. But I've been listening this whole time.

I taught for 12 years, he says. I've got a master's degree, a bunch of awards, job offers.

I just want you to know, he says, everything this woman says is true.

Everything.

So I wait tables.

Engaged to the ugliest woman on the planet...

S he'd been a receptionist for the newspaper for decades. She had a feeling something was wrong. So she knocked on my door.

Take a look at this picture.

Imagine the ugliest woman you've ever seen. Multiply it by 10. This face was scary bad. A cold chill down your spine kind of face.

"Somebody just brought by a wedding announcement. This is the bride. The groom is a county deputy. He didn't bring it. The girl didn't bring it. Usually, it's one or the other. And this is the crappiest photograph anybody ever submitted."

Just to be on the safe side, we came up with a plan. Our suspicious receptionist would casually stop by the sheriff's office, get a new signature from the groom.

That's when the fun started.

The photograph of the woman... the record-breaking, mirror-breaking ugliest woman in the world... actually was the property of the Department of Corrections. Said female was under sentence of death for a series of murders. Very nasty murders.

And so the wedding announcement was a prank. End of story? Not hardly.

This one took some investigating to put together.

The would-be victim of the gnarly wedding announcement was actually due for some payback, for a stunt he'd pulled.

It began with the new guy on the force. Night shift. Checking doors. This guy would drive around, stop at offices and closed-up stores, park the cruiser, walk to the door and rattle the knob. For eight hours.

First night, the one door he'd never again want to see. The old courthouse.

Set well back from the road. Surrounded by grandfather oaks. Side door. Long brick walkway, bordered on both sides by a hedge about 10 feet high. Streetlight, busted for the occasion.

It's pitch black.

Picture a couple of guys hiding at the end of this walkway. And I don't know how they managed this part, but they had succeeded in persuading a local tourist trap to lend them their gator. A very old, very stuffed, very big gator.

I'd seen this thing myself, in its commercial habitat. It was Old Florida, mebbe 16 feet long. You could cram basketballs inside his gaping jaws.

So here's the newbie, walking down the narrow pathway between the towering hedges. Guy's probably thinking about Stephen King right now.

He gets to the end of the walkway, hears a guttural moan. Steps closer.

Moan turns into a growl.

Big Boy comes flying at him out of the darkness.

Newbie cop did not draw his weapon. He did not call for backup. He did not demand to see some ID.

This sucker ran as fast and as far as he could, leaving behind his own cruiser, a dead gator and a couple of guys laughing so hard they coulda been heard across town.

Legend has it newbie then stopped by the house to change pants.

His revenge plot had style, but it fell short when he selected a lover just too ugly to be believed.

Otherwise, the lead perp of this conspiracy might have found himself "engaged" to a sweet young thing destined for the electric chair.

Take us to some voodoo…

Spent the day talking to bureaucrats in Port au Prince about the plight of the Haitians, about why somebody with zero education would try to climb into a leaky homemade boat the size of a bathtub and try to make it to Florida. Wind, waves, sharks, heat.

And, if you get caught trying to leave, mebbe a bullet. One for you. More for anyone in your family.

Everywhere, there are kids hawking carved dolls, jewelry and trinkets, moms carrying baskets of brightly colored cloth on their heads. Dads pissing in the street.

Stench. Despair.

Long day.

It's dark. Two of us. We come out of the hotel. Lots of guys offering lots of things. But one guy's got a big Chevy Caprice. We hand him a twenty.

Take us to some voodoo.

He drives through town, outa town, long past the paved road. Now we're just meandering through the woods, no road, we serpentine around the trees. Long time goes by. Then, we can hear the drums. A clearing near the water.

A guy walks out.

What do you want?

We open our wallets. He smiles.

We're sitting around the circle. It's made of fine sand. There are six guys, totally ripped, hitting clubs on hollowed logs. Faster than you can count, harder than you can imagine. They are indescribably impressive. Most guys I know could do this for about three minutes. These guys may never stop.

Women sing, dance frenetically across the circle. Pass rum. One appears to bite the head off a live chicken. Not sure, though. Could be some kinda stunt. But this is real: A couple guys are tearing burning coals from firebrands with their teeth.

In the midst of it all, a young girl is making an intricate design in the sand, pouring salt between her thumb and forefinger. Her work is incredible.

Beyond the light of the fires, we can see a round building with a thatched roof, right against the water. We have to get onto our hands and knees to crawl through a tiny opening to get inside.

Immediately, my head is spinning. There's something in there. Dope... decaying something... maybe just air that's generations old. A sandy floor around a fire pit, masks, drawings on the wall, carvings. I stay inside long enough to look around, then stagger back through the crawl space.

The dancing is full bore now, dozens of people jammed tight against each other, leaping, shaking their heads from side to side, tongues lolling.

Finally we go.

In the morning, along the street, there are raw fish and vegetables for sale, covered in a dense carpet of flies. It's close to 100 degrees.

I meet a Catholic priest who shows me an orphanage full of tuberculosis and conjunctivitis. I say I've seen it in half the faces since I've been here.

Everyone has it, he says.

We walk. Behind a small house, two men are building a boat.

Write your obit before you leave...

I t was a court proceeding in a weird drug case. Woman loved to get high on coke, especially by injection. Problem was, she had an intense fear of needles.

So she'd go out with some friends. They'd hold her down and shoot her up. And the hold her down part was for real. She would put up a fight with everything she had.

A judge was gonna decide whether the fact that she died after one of these little parties was purely an accidental overdose, or whether her buddies oughta be charged with manslaughter.

Their defense: It was what she wanted. Prosecutor: This is some nasty stuff and somebody needs to go away for awhile.

Judge agreed. The party gang got held over for trial.

So I write about what a sinister thing it is for a drug to be so enchanting that someone would subject themselves to their worst fear to enjoy it. And keep doing it.

I get a phone call the next day from a guy who says the dead girl was his sister. And he does not appreciate the fact that I held up her dirty laundry for everybody to read about. He's pretty pissed. Says he's gonna shoot me with his new deer rifle.

He proceeds to tell me what kinda car I drive and where I live. He is correct on both counts. At the time, I lived a good ways outa town, no listed phone, etc. Mebbe he's been following me.

I try to reason with him, no luck. So I hang up. Guy who sits next to me has overheard some of this, asks what it was all about. I tell him.

Then I go to lunch. When I get back, my boss calls me into his office.

What's this about a death threat?

Not a big deal, I say. Guy's pretty upset right now. It'll blow over.

But my boss is totally pissed off. Don't you ever get a death threat without telling me about it, he says.

No big deal, I say.

I'm not concerned about your frickin safety, he says.

I want you to write your obit before you leave.

You're about to lose an arm...

A nother story from that circus that was holed up for the winter. This was in the boonies in Central Florida. The Clyde Beatty show.

I'm out walking around among tents and cages, tigers roaring, monkeys chattering. I'm looking for a good story. Amid tractor trailers, railroad cars, scaffolding, I see a guy sitting on a bench, wrangling with a wrench on some kinda broken gimcrack. Next to him are two rows of cages. Inside, buncho tigers. Big ones.

There's an aisle between the cages about three feet wide. I'm talking to this guy. He's one of these guys who takes some time to think about what he's gonna say. Then he takes some time saying it.

I just wanna know where the people are who run the place, the people who decide when it's time to let the lions and the tigers and the elephants and the monkeys sit still.

He's telling me who, where to find em, what it's like being off the road. What it's like being on the road.

Then, casually... "You're about to lose an arm there, fella."

I'm standing next to a tiger, Bengal mebbe. About the size of a Jeep. I'm looking at the tiger. He's looking at me.

"We don't walk between the cages," he says. "We go around."

Says the tiger is real fast. Pretty sure the guy's laughing at me, or he should be.

Either way.

How to tell when politicians are lying...

I t's when their mouths are open.

This is in Beaufort, South Carolina. Folks here are begging Georgia Democrat Jimmy Carter to stop by. Carter 's running for president. He can't make it.

But Walter Mondale can come. Not long from now, this senator from Minnesota will become the vice president. Folks here are pretty excited, so they lay on a big shrimp boil. Mondale's late arriving, but he makes up for it with sirens.

Pictures. Handshakes. Pictures.

Finally, Mondale gets to sit. People address him as Mr. Vice President. He smiles.

Now... we haven't had an election just yet, he says.

Then... disaster.

You can picture us all sitting there, frantically looking back and forth at each other.

Did I just see what I thought?

The senator is putting shrimp right into his mouth and crunching down on em. I say crunching because Mr. Mondale ain't peeling the shrimp. He's just eating em. He's working his teeth over THE TAILS! Looking around to see if it's ok to pull the tails back out of his mouth.

Delicious, he says.

Mighty fine.

Who's gonna handle this!?

Local politico—mighta been the mayor, or mebbe it was the head of the local Democratic party—quietly taps the senator on the arm.

Sir, he begins. Just one moment... please. The senator pauses.

Those shrimp. Those shrimp are unpeeled, sir.

The man was not prepared for this. Frankly, neither man was prepared for this.

Aah, says the senator.

In a few moments, an eager diplomat across the table has instructed him on shrimp peeling. Two swipes, once you get good at it. Mr. Mondale carefully peels his first shrimp. Puts it in his mouth.

Aah, he says.

Very good. I like em even better this way.

It was so horrific; the jurors were holding their hands over their ears...

K ind of a tossup to decide who was the nastiest guy behind bars in Florida. But a lotta votes would go for Freddy Goode.

Freddy molested a couple of little boys and murdered them. There were other assaults too, over the years, but it was those killings that got Freddy the electric chair.

Freddy sent gruesome letters to the parents, describing in detail what he'd done. He told the judge he was glad to be sentenced to death, because, if they let him out, he'd grab more youngsters.

Freddy liked pushing people's buttons. At his trial, he insisted on handling his own defense. That was just so he could brag some more, taunt some people.

Some of the jurors held their hands over their ears.

Lot of people despised him. They put him on death row at Florida State Prison, not only because he earned it, but because he'd be safer there.

Freddy's dad once told me it was obvious the kid was a nasty wackjob early on. His third grade teacher sent a note home, calling the kid "frightening" and asking what would happen if he committed horrible crimes someday and got off by pleading mental illness.

Third grade.

Freddy spent time in hospitals and rehab. People kept letting him out. Then one night, his dad was watching tv, saw the news about a local kid who'd been raped and murdered. He stormed into his son's room and accused him of it. He was shouting so loudly, the next-door neighbor heard it and called 911.

That's how Freddy got caught.

He gleefully told the cops... "You can't do anything to me... I'm sick."

I wanted to make a surprise visit to the prison one time. Ordinarily, newspaper people had to ask for permission. I didn't want to give them time to dust off the place. So I called Bobby Brantley, a state legislator, asked him if he'd ride up there with me, so we could just stroll through the gate.

We're walking down the hall on Death Row. Freddy spots the guy and yells out to him. He'd recognized his face.

"Aren't you that state lawmaker?" he says. "You can do anything you want, right?"

Brantley wasn't real comfortable talking with Freddy, but he walked over to the cell when Freddy said there was something urgent he needed to tell him.

Freddy whispered.

"Can you get me some little boys? Maybe just one? For a little while?"

Now Brantley's walking away, shaking his head.

"You don't understand..." Freddy yells after us. "I'm stuck in here."

Bike Week— Daytona Beach... It's us vs. them...

Bike Week in Daytona Beach. Thousands of guys and their hogs. And their bikes. This is about as much fun as you will ever have.

Leather, fumes, dope, beards, boots, swastikas, tattoos, roaring exhausts, people staggering, people yelling, people taunting.

I am with a guy who has a reputation for saying exactly the wrong thing at the wrong time. For outdoing himself. This will be a significant factor in the day.

Right now, we are talking to people, taking pictures, taking it all in.

We come upon a custom Harley that is the finest of the custom Harleys that crowd the street. It's gold and chrome and tricked out like you wouldn't believe. It is stunning. My friend is taking pictures of it.

Along comes a woman. I can tell this because she has practically no clothes on. She says it's her bike, actually, her man's bike. She climbs aboard and proceeds to display herself across the handlebars and the seat. She's had a few drinks. She's feeling pretty good. And warm. She's feeling very warm.

She begins to remove the last of her clothing. Turns to the camera. Smiles.

My gracious and well-mannered associate proceeds to tell her to get her large unappealing derriere off the frickin bike while he's trying to photograph it. He does not say it nicely.

He sees only the bike. I see a guy.

He's mebbe 6'5"... 350. And he's coming fast.

I grab my buddy. We run, pushing our way into the Boot Hill Saloon, the most famous biker bar in the city.

You thought it was intense on the street.

My buddy soon decides the best picture is a wide-angle from above; in this case, from a vantage point atop the bar. It seems like a great idea, the only objections coming from the bartender holding the Louisville Slugger, the two guys my friend has just drenched in beer and the women whose pitcher my friend dumped on the aforementioned guys. And all the pissed-off drunk bikers who are now calling him names.

You think he's gonna take that kinda grief? Hell no. After all, he's got me. And there's only 200 or so of them. So he cusses em out. All of em.

I tell him he's on his own and bolt for the door. He follows.

Not completely under his own steam.

This guy wants to bring three moving vans full of stuff to Florida... wants you to pay...

A guy gets a job offer in Orlando. He's in Indiana. So his new boss, the University of Central Florida, offers to pay his moving bill.

Little did they know.

Here's a guy who thought he needed a snow shovel in Central Florida. And a bunch of other stuff you wouldn't believe.

The moving van shows up. It gets filled. Then another. Then another. Three big trucks.

The list of stuff went on for 31 pages. Six picnic tables, rabbit pens.

A plow.

Reminds me of carting a two-year to grandma's for the summer.

Somebody in Tallahassee saw the bill and said no. The university asked for an exception. It was only 57,560 pounds of stuff.

But the state auditor refused, said it looked like the guy had made "little effort to minimize..."

What did the guy have to say?

He didn't think his household was especially large.

Everybody needs two swing sets, no? And nine desks. Did I mention... 20 bicycles?

And a bale of hay.

Thousands gather outside window of a paralyzed cop...

L istening to FM in Miami one morning. The jock starts talking about a young woman who's just been shot.

She's a police officer who was driving home to her apartment complex when she spooked some guys in the middle of a break-in. Now she's paralyzed, inches from death. People start calling in to the radio station, talking about how they need this woman to pull through. Talking about life in the city... crime... endurance...

The station quits playing music. Hundreds of people are calling.

Shootings are not rare here. But as the word spreads, the switchboard at Baptist Hospital starts to jam. People are calling to offer money for her care. If she lives, she may be confined to a wheelchair for the rest of her life. At the radio station, people are knocking on the door, leaving money. Crime victims from cases she'd handled long ago call in crying.

The outrage is building.

Off-duty cops are showing up in droves. Guys finish their shifts and keep working. Cheryl Seiden drove a charcoal gray RX7.

The shooter stole it. Now cops are pulling them over, so many of them, half a dozen stolen charcoal gray RX7s get recovered.

A woman who drives one gets stopped seven times. People are calling the cops: I just saw one of those cars.

Friends of the radio jock finally drive him home. He's been on the air taking calls for 26 hours straight.

The docs say Seiden is barely hanging on. People begin to assemble outside her window. This vigil will grow from hundreds of people to thousands. The entire city is calling out to her to live.

Five days after the shooting, cops get a tip about a car in a canal. It's hers. They arrest two guys and charge them with attempted murder. One of the guys agrees to testify against the other in exchange for a lighter sentence.

The shooter will get life.

As for Seiden, she hung on for two weeks. In that time, she was not able to communicate. But she understood. She knew what people were doing for her.

This guy knows he's gonna die, and it will take about 20 minutes...

You spend any time at all in a big room that has a cop scanner and you get to where you can tell right away if it's important. There's a tone of voice, adrenalin mebbe.

A guy is working on a crew digging a ditch alongside a road, putting in a big sewer line. There's been a cave-in. He's half buried.

They're sending everybody.

This guy has been working inside one of those massive metal safety barriers, the thing with the big walls on either side of the guys working in the hole.

But Florida's got some stuff that's like quicksand, or worse. It sucks you down and keeps you.

As soon as this guy was in the clutches, his team jumped in there with shovels and buckets. No good. They tried a backhoe. No good. They tried pumping the stuff out. No good. They tried tying a rope under his shoulders and lifting him out. It was tearing him in half.

He was huge. And the suction was too great.

We're talking dozens of guys, broad daylight, every kind of equipment you can imagine. They can't get him out. Construction guys throwing their hard hats on the ground and bursting into tears.

Finally a guy got down there next to him with a pad and a pen. He wrote, as the guy dictated his will, his final messages to his family.

They kept trying until the end.

A family comes to grips with the unthinkable...

A family on the coast, their little boy, kidnapped. Someone grabbed him after school.

It's still sketchy. The cops aren't sure, but it is unimaginably frightening.

Who knows why they agreed to this. But we had a writer who knew the parents. She was one of those sympathetic, genuine people who could talk to anybody about anything. So she asked them: What if one of our people came to stay with you?

For the next three days, Cory Jo Lancaster will live with the family. She'll be there when the phone rings, when the police come, when they learn the truth.

It began with a photo in the local paper. Junny Rios-Martinez, a blond-headed, 11-year-old in a surfer's t-shirt. Later, there was a message on the phone. A reporter thought the kid might make a good story. He showed up to talk. He had a photo ID.

Eventually, he would say he was no longer a newspaper reporter, that he'd left for a better job with a surfing magazine. And, now, he could probably get the kid some bling, maybe even some endorsements.

He ran a long string and the parents bought it.

The kid would get some money up-front. There'd be some travel. There were contracts to sign.

The boy's mom didn't feel completely right about it, but it seemed ok. The writer, Mark Dean was his name, always knew the right thing to say to put them at ease.

But they had some final questions. They needed to be sure. So they told Mark to come back.

That was the day their boy disappeared.

The cops didn't know any Mark Dean. But they did know Mark Dean Schwab. And now the fear began to set in.

Schwab was just out of prison for molesting a kid. A kid he brought him home afterward.

The cops have a photo of Schwab. It's him. Schwab's been free for just three weeks, after serving three years of an eight-year sentence.

Cory Jo is there while the parents talk about their worst fears. She's there as the phone rings, over and over and over again. Neighbors. Family. Police.

Night comes and goes. No one sleeps.

An FBI agent arrives. He'll stay for days. His presence makes it all the more real. The fears are inescapable. The parents tell themselves... he'll bring our boy back. Dad burns through cigarettes and Pepsi. Mom wants to talk with a psychic.

One guy knew all along it was too good to be true. A 12-year-old, the best friend. He kept saying, there's no way this is for real.

Cops are in and out. Their faces tell the tale. The FBI guy's advice—stop answering the phone. Get all these people out of here.

Hope, revulsion, emptiness, images of agonizing violence. What if he has AIDS?

A crisis counselor takes the parents into a back room.

It's been four days now. Mom sits on her son's bed, staring at the posters on the wall, the framed photo of him in that surfer shirt, the one that started all this.

Then the police call. They've got Schwab.

He's alone.

It will be another two days before he leads police to the foot-locker. Middle of the night, in a downpour, he relents, shows them the truth.

Cory Jo will quietly leave the house. In a few days, there will be a funeral and more than 1,500 people will be there.

Schwab was executed. Florida passed a law that prohibits molesters from getting early release. They named the law after little Junny.

She died the instant she saw her daughter's body...

L ittle town in Florida called Brooksville, where the houses sit close to the edge of the road. The kind of place where not much happens, and when it does, everybody talks about it.

So it was no surprise when folks got up and ran outside one night when they heard a wreck down the street. A couple of people got deputized to investigate. A 14-year-old girl named Karen, a few others. Karen wanted to be a nurse, sang in the chorus, had just bought her first dress.

The wreck was minor. It was late. The cops weren't there yet. Somebody was out in the road with a flashlight, warning people to slow down. The cars in the fender bender had their flashers on. No one was expecting more trouble.

Then another car came roaring out of the darkness, moving fast, way too fast. The driver, a young kid, swerved to miss the jumble of cars. He'd been drinking.

Later, the cops would say... this is why we chase people away from accident scenes.

The kid's car went up on the shoulder, airborne, hit a parked car. The crowd scattered.

But not that 14-year-old.

Back at the house, her mom was waiting. Heart trouble, diabetes, high blood pressure. Couldn't work, but she loved to tinker in the garden.

The wreck was only a block away. Her daughter should have been home by now. It was all taking too long.

Mom went down. There was an ambulance, a lot of people crowded around the body. They held her back, but she could see.

They heard her scream.

"It's my daughter."

She took a long deep breath and fell backward.

The old woman had 50 dogs... said they were no trouble...

G ot a call from a guy who lived near a woman who had dozens and dozens of dogs. All of em, living inside a trailer.

He was calling the cops, which he'd done a few times. But the guy was actually pretty sympathetic.

Maybe, he said, there's something you can do.

I made my way from the driveway to the front door, which was not easy. The grass and the weeds were tangled, up to my waist. Couldn't see the ground.

I knocked. We talked awhile. She didn't want to invite me in, but she did, eventually. There was not a single place to step without getting it all over my shoes. There was no place to sit without getting it all over me. The stench was overwhelming. The noise, deafening. There was no way to count. They kept moving. But there could have been 50. That was her guess.

Some of them had jumped up on the countertops, like cats.

They're no trouble, she said. No trouble at all. She said they never went to the bathroom inside. They were all trained. She would send them out in shifts and call them in, she said.

I'm gonna find homes for em. I just have a few that I'm real attached to.

Which ones, I asked?

That one and that one and that one and that one and that one. She wore a big bathrobe. Sadly, she hadn't been able to find a place to sit either. She was old and she had hair that hung longer on one side and she was nervous.

Sometimes, she'd put papers on the floor. And then she'd carry em outside and burn em in a big barrel.

I could see the barrel in the backyard.

Later, I drove around the corner to the next street, stopped in to see the guy who'd called me. Nice place. Landscaping.

We walked outside to his back yard, to the pool. It was filled with ash, blown over the fence from her place.

The racket was pretty bad out here.

We have to keep the door shut, he said. And nobody in my family will go in the pool.

I wanted to go back, talk to her some more, but I didn't. It just seemed like putting on a good face for company was more than she could bear.

Later on, he sent me a note. The health department had come out, with the animal control people. They'd left a few dogs with her, as many as the law would allow. She'd tried to pick out a few, I guess. But a lot of them were sick. I could picture it. It would have been her worst day.

They sent some people out to help her clean up the place. Somebody cut the grass for her. The neighbors were going to see what they could do.

It wasn't the first time they'd tried. Before long, there would be more.

Are you insane? You can't drive that truck in here...!

W e have so many writers and photographers covering this next shuttle launch we need two big RVs to carry us all.

I get recruited to drive because this thing is about 500 feet long and nobody else wants to mess with it. It's real big, real slow and you sit about roof-high. So we jam everybody inside, turn up the radio, stop for hot dogs, beer and potato chips. We're gonna get there early so we need energy to keep going.

And these people are pretty excited. They've seen launches. They know what it's like.

Remember when you put a firecracker under a beer can?

The can would pop up high into the air. But then it would fall. Not so this thing. After three minutes it will be a tiny glint in the sky, traveling 6,200 feet per second.

It's the most ambitious technological undertaking in history. But this technology's more delicate, less forgiving, than life.

Why you need all those writers. They're specialists. Science experts.

Engine problems, tiles falling off, insulation peeling, temperature fluctuations, power surges, phantom readouts. It seems like most of the time, the Mission Control guys just have to stop, start over, push reset.

But this day, as they make final preparations, the sun is shining. Not a problem in the world.

I pull up to the toll booth.

The guy just stares at me, eyes bulging, jaw hanging. He gets out of the booth. Walks to the front of the vehicle. Now there are two or three other toll guys there. They've left their booths. They're walking to the sides of the RV, looking. Talking to each other like a clique of NFL refs.

Something wrong?

This lane is not for trucks. He's shouting now.

You can't pull trucks in here.

Sorry. How much do I owe you?

You don't understand. Still shouting.

You have about 1/8 of an inch on either side here. This lane is for cars. It is frickin unbelievable you got this thing in here without bashing the booth.

But they're laughing now. A great story for the gang at the bar tonight. They take our money. We leave. No big deal.

Tell that to Peter Larson. I think it was Larson, the guy driving the other RV. The one right behind me.

He proceeds to wedge that puppy in between a couple of toll booths so tight he can't move. He tries backing up, going forward again, as if he was stuck in the mud. He does this a whole bunch of times. The agonizing shriek of metal against brick. He's shredding the sides of the truck, from bumper to bumper, tearing off the mirrors.

He finally gets it free. And it looks just like you'd expect it to.

Later, we need to take these fancy high-priced trucks back to the dealer.

Is there a place with big bushes we can park next to?
We drive to the back of the lot. Wave to the folks in the office.
Thanks again.
Let the boss handle this one.

Escape from China...

H e was older now, a generation away from the day he'd escaped. He was willing to tell me his story, but only if I agreed not to print it. Tell me, I said.

It began when they were boys. Two youngsters living in Fukien Province, the part of mainland China closest to Taiwan. Every day, after the sun set, they swam in the river near their house, training for the time they would dare attempt the 24-hour endurance test that could bring them freedom. It was 80 miles. Or more.

Every night... winter, spring, summer, fall, rain or shine, cold, hot.

For more than 10 years, they swam. They grew tall and strong. And then they began to swim in the strait. They knew how long it would take, how long to reach the midpoint, the place at which they would just have to keep going.

That night, the waters were calm. They said goodbye to their families and began. They were nearing the point of no return when his boyhood friend called out to him. He'd lost his nerve.

I can't make it, he said. I'm going back.

He went on alone. After a time, he made it to New York, where he got work in a restaurant. He learned the trade. For years, he worked. And then he had his own restaurant. He'd done enough that he let someone else run it for him.

But every time a new restaurant opened nearby, he went in. He tried the elaborate dishes, the things that were difficult to get right. If anyone surprised him, he'd walk into the kitchen, introduce himself.

And then one day, he sampled something that caught his fancy. It was chicken, a nice sauce, something delicate. He walked into the kitchen, asked if he could meet the chef.

The man had his back to him. And then he turned. They began to shake, to cry. Stunned, they embraced. Decades later. Thousands and thousands of miles later. The boy who had gone back had not given up. He'd tried again, the next year.

They had ended up in the same country, the same state, the same city, the same occupation. The same skills.

But you cannot tell anyone, he said to me. People would never come to my restaurant if they thought I was a communist.

In this country, people will think you are a hero, I told him.

I cannot take the chance.

It was his choice.

How to date a witch... three easy steps...

Woman calls me one day, says a reporter has been rude to her... agonizingly rude.

I listen to her story, commiserate. She cools down. Then she warms up, to me.

You're a very sympathetic personality, she says. It's obvious you're a Pisces. Mister Rude, he's a Taurus. No question.

I hang up. I call the rude guy, John Glisch, who is actually one of the more courteous folks in our line.

Hey man, you a Taurus?

He is. And I'm a Pisces.

Whatev... chalk it up.

Next day, I get a call from the receptionist on the first floor. A woman has just delivered an envelope. I go down, grab it.

Inside, an invitation. From her.

One thing I forgot to mention. She's a witch. She told me so. Wiccan.

Asked me how I felt about it. Fine with me, I said.

Anyhow, she's decided that she and I have a thing. Because of the phone call. We're connected. And now she wants to proceed, take the next step.

But she's playing it cool. Wants me to initiate. How that's gonna happen is spelled out in the letter.

If you want to see me again, she says, just take a spider's leg, put it in a glass of water, hold it up to the full moon, look at the moon through the glass (of water, with spider leg) and, boom, the phone number will appear.

Imagine my disappointment. Could not for the life of me remember where I put all the spider legs.

It's pitch black. His hands are shaking. He points. They're right behind you.

There's an obituary about a guy who died right after his wife. They'd been married for something like 63 years. So you think, here's a case where they spent their entire lives together. They didn't wanna live apart. So I drive out there. See if I can write about it. I'm walking from the street to the house— it's one of those old Florida ranch styles, a one-story brick place that sits about 50 yards off a small lake. The next door neighbor comes out, introduces himself.

We begin to talk. He loved these guys, best friends, knew em for decades. He's filling my notebook with stories about how they met, how they courted, their lives. They used to sit on a bench in the afternoons and look at the water.

Asks me if I'd like to look around inside. We go in the back door. He's grieving and it helps to talk about it. So he does. For hours.

I'm grateful. They sound like wonderful people. But it's time to go. It's getting dark. We're sitting there in the den of this empty old house and he's just getting warmed up. Emotional. Remembering the time. Now the sun's gone. It's pitch black in this house and he's whispering now, tears streaming and there's not a light on in the place.

He can't believe they're gone. He thinks mebbe they haven't gone, not completely. He talks about their plans. How they wanted to be together, not just in life, but after.

Barely audible now. And then he looks up, lifts a shaky hand, points just over my shoulder. A catch in his voice.

"They're right behind you...."

I stand, naturally. Move a little bit—away. It's the fireplace. There's an urn over the mantle.

Time to go.

And then the boom brushed against the power line…

It was windy and I was about to be two and half hours late for dinner.

It started in the late afternoon. Construction site, guys putting girders together for an office building. There was a guy working the big crane. The steel was long, heavy. Two guys on the ground would attach the choker cables, then back off while he lifted it free.

He'd pluck that girder off the stack, swing it around. When he had it stabilized, they'd step back in, grab hold of the ends . A bit of do-si-do… swinging the I-beam around. Then a slow lift to the riveters.

Somebody should have seen this coming.

The wind came up. You wouldn't think it would affect something that big, that heavy.

Side pull, they call it. The guy working the crane was looking down, not up. The boom brushed against the power line. Too close for that kind of work.

Now the girder was hot. And when the first guy came in to steady it, he died the instant he put his hand on the beam. I heard what happened, made some calls, talked to people who'd been there, the police, the ambulance driver. Then I sent in the story.

And now it was late. A typical Florida night. Breezy, but warm. We were sitting on the deck of my friend's place, one of those duplexes standing on stilts, with the parking slab underneath. I was telling the story.

We saw the car coming, weaving all over the road. It was the guy who rented the other half of the duplex. He got the car most of the way into the driveway. The door opened and he fell out onto the ground.

We went down to help. He could barely stand. He saw us, started to babble. He was sobbing and yelling and nothing made sense.

We started carrying him up the stairs. And finally we could understand him.

I just killed a guy, he said. Shouting now.

You know anybody who needs a crane operator who kills people?

Then he stood tall and pushed us away. He couldn't get the key in the door, so he smashed the glass and reached in to open it.

We heard dishes breaking and stuff smashing against a wall. And then it was quiet.

He'd sent more men to the electric chair...

The old solicitor was a guy named Buster Murdaugh. Buster was a white-headed, seersuckered, aw-shucks country lawyer who'd sent more men to the electric chair than anyone in South Carolina history. There were some who said he'd sent more men to the chair than anybody, anywhere.

But this time was different. Buster was so outraged by the savagery of the murder two Yankee hitchhikers had committed he told the jury he'd quit the business if they didn't give them the juice. He wasn't going to work in the criminal justice system any longer if people like that could walk free.

The jury wasted little time giving them both a death sentence. Then the lawyers for the killers mounted an appeal.

But I'm getting ahead of myself.

That day in the street, Buster was still mulling his speech to the jury. And those two men hadn't yet made it to the courthouse.

They would come in the back way, through the lane. That way no one would see them. They wouldn't even come in a car. They'd walk, sneak in through the back door.

I knew where to wait. I was there with a photographer, Fred Rollison, and we saw them coming. Fred had a telephoto, started shooting as soon as they got around the corner, out from behind the trees.

The detective in front, tough guy, despised the press. We'd had run-ins before.

"Put that camera down," he shouted. "Put that camera down or go to jail." Fred dropped his hands.

"Public street," I said. "Keep shooting."

And he did. The deputies sprinted for us, shouting threats. The first two grabbed Fred, tore the camera from around his neck, lifted him nearly off his feet, yanking him in a headlock toward the building. He backhanded me the other camera, the smaller one he kept over his shoulder. I started shooting.

And then they had both of us inside. More shouts, cursing. They'd taken the cameras. One of the deputies started to open the back, ruin the film.

"Stop right there," I said. "Before this gets any worse. Stop. Call your boss. Tell him you're arresting us. Tell him we're in the street."

"I'm not calling anybody. You're going to jail."

"This is about to be a real problem for you," I said.

He made the call. A moment later, handed me the cameras. Apologized, the words forced from the back of his throat, past a mouthful of hate.

That day, his picture ran in every paper in the state. The picture I took of him dragging Fred up the stairs.

Inside, Buster stormed across the courtroom, raised his hands in the air and roared at the jury. Around his neck, he had draped the garden hose they had used to strangle the victim. Wore it for hours.

It was reminiscent of the trial where he'd spent days parading about the courtroom holding the murder weapon, taunting the defendant, sneering, and then, finally getting him on the stand

and pushing him to brink, thrusting the gun toward him, shouting: "Show us how you killed him!"

The poor man lunged for the weapon with a snarl. "This thing better not be loaded."

But on this day, Buster summed up with this: Give these killers the chair, or I won't ever again practice law.

And that was why he lost. The defense lawyers said it was too much pressure to put on a jury. Nobody wanted to be responsible for the premature retirement of the legend that was Buster Murdaugh.

New trial was ordered. Same result. Bad guys got the chair.

Glenn Miller chases the chill from the air...

It was freezing outside and they couldn't have cared less.

The auditorium, as big as an airplane hangar. Inside, the legendary Glenn Miller Orchestra was chasing the chill from the air with a pulsating blast of swing that took hold, wouldn't let go.

New faces carrying on the name, some of 'em kinda baby-faced. Everybody in the place had heard those tunes when they were brand new. But as soon as the music started the crowd knew. The big band was back.

In an instant, the dance floor bulged with couples shedding the years as they'd shed their overcoats coming in the door. White-headed ladies with their hair just so, sporting bracelets and beads and crinkly smiles they'd been saving up. Dapper gents carefully spinning, cooing into their ears. "We're going to Michigan to see the sweetest gal, from Kalamazoo—zoo—zoo—zoo—zoo."

Dressed to the nines. Elegant.

Slapping time on the tables, shuffling their feet back and forth in front of their chairs. Infection sweeping the room.

A woman scarcely taller than a doorknob came up to me, grinning.

"You can dance to that Glenn miller, I tell you."

Sporting a new print dress. She and a girlfriend had come by themselves.

"We knew we'd find some partners."

Fond memories, full of life. Old picnic tables and paper tablecloths. They didn't care.

Loud. Slick. Biting chromatic harmonies in the brass, punching countermelodies, snapping crescendos. The trombones shunting from side to side. Trumpets soaring, saxes tearing into their solos.

Singers cupping tiny megaphones to imitate the tinny radio sound of bygone years got a roomful of applause every time they strode toward the microphones.

Blue hairs strutting, slapping their hands.

And then their favorite... "In the mood..."

The horns building it, layer after layer. People leaping up to dance in the aisles and in the back of the room.

One old guy stood next to me, looking like he'd burst if he stopped moving. And looking slightly terrified.

"Man, there are some good dancers out there."

"Little Brown Jug," "Stardust," Tuxedo Junction," The St. Louis Blues March," "Mack the Knife."

It went on for four hours. In between songs, they'd stay on the dance floor, waiting.

And then it was time. They bent over to fetch their furs and hats and, clinging to each other's arms, they made their way back into the cold night air, leaving behind clouds of perfume, echoes of better days.

A woman heading for the door saw me smiling and pranced over, collared me with a hug, bursting with it.

"We senior citizens do a lot of *wild things*."

Singing as she left.

"Don't sit under the apple tree, with anyone else but me..."

First there's love... then an explosion...

Driving out to the Cape for a launch in a big RV. Maybe five of us. The launch has been delayed several times, tech glitches. We may be here awhile.

So it's evening, we're inside the trailer. Couple of pizzas, case of beer. There's a pull-down bunk that hangs over the front windshield. Bob, the guy in it, used to be a political front-man, the guy who arrives a few days before the candidate to set up appearances, logistics.

His real creds: He used to drive a taxicab.

Now he's a writer. Gonna see his first launch.

The thing we do not know right now is that the bunk is not locked into its supports. It's just resting against the front windshield visors, which are almost the size of the front windshield and which are sticking out, when they're supposed to be tucked outa the way before—you get the picture.

Sitting in the passenger side chair is a young lady who thinks Taxi is pretty hot stuff. Evening goes on, she has more beer than is good for her, she begins to think Taxi is Real Hot Stuff. She's working herself up to the big moment.

It arrives. She climbs up on the arms of the chair, launches skyward and, for the briefest moment, she's suspended there, in bed, alongside the man of her dreams.

WHHOOSH.

Windshield explodes.

Screaming.

The launch goes as scheduled. Bit of luck.

Next day, I'm driving this thing down the interstate, no windshield, just bits of glass occasionally flying back into the vehicle. I get back to the office. I'm telling my boss about the 18-wheeler that careened passed us on the highway, about the big old *chunk of gravel* that flew up into the windshield as we drove down the road.

Good guy. Sense of humor. Let's me wax. Tragic event, I say. Insurance will have to cover it.

He pats me on the arm.

She's already been in, he says. She confessed.

But that was a good story you told.

They find that body yet...?

O ld woman disappears. Very strange case.

People saw her buy groceries. They saw her heading out, on foot. Everybody knew her. She was there at the store every week. Most of the time, somebody gave her a ride.

This day, she never made it home. The local constables do not wanna talk about this. At all.

Something weird going on here.

Time passes. I write about how there is still no explanation for the disappearance and still no information forthcoming from the people who get paid to solve this stuff. This does not endear me to the guys in uniform.

One morning, phone rings and it's a woman who lives near the highway. She wants to know: Where are all the cops going? Tons of em and they are screaming up the road.

The only thing out past her house is a state park. Nobody out there, except a ranger who lives in a cabin.

I wish this next thing was my idea. But it belongs to a guy who was my editor for awhile. Long-timer who quit newspapers to become a private detective. Had a suspicious mind.

I call the park ranger. I have just one question. My tone of voice says I'm in on the thing. I know all about it. I am casual.

"They find the body yet?"

He proceeds to lay it all out for me. How they've been search-ing all night with every dog in the county. How they seemed to know what they were looking for, where to look. Which is right where they found her, tossed in some bushes not far from the side of the road.

Very nasty. Whoever did this committed five or six acts of violence on this poor woman, any of which would have been more than enough.

My story hits the streets before the officers get back to town.

Chief of detectives calls me up. Loud. Livid.

Where'd you get all that stuff?

Is it wrong? I ask.

"No, you dirty frickin S.O.B."

I have just, he says, burned my last bridge. I will never get one ounce of cooperation on anything for the rest of my life.

How, I ask, is that different from, say, yesterday?

He slams down the phone. I drive into town, so he can spot me walking down the hallway past his office.

That might be the dead boy's mom, out there on the dance floor...

A major high school athlete is killed in a hit and run. Kid was walking across an unlit street. Killed instantly.

I drive out to the house. His uncle is there. He can't talk right now, he's got to get ready.

People are coming over. Bunch of people. I ask if it's all right if I stick around and talk to some family and friends.

Help yourself. Budweisers in the cooler.

This kid was going to be highly recruited. A class kid, good grades, good citizen, great work ethic, bushel of talent. A kid worth writing about.

Within 30 minutes, the house is full. I take some notes. Talk to a few people. But it's not easy. They're getting pretty loud. And it's hard to catch people.

They're jumping up to get another drink. They're jumping up to dance. They've got the furniture all moved out of the way now.

Motown on the boombox. It's cranking.

Fried chicken. But mostly it's Crown Royal with beer chasers. Some of these family and friends are getting pretty toasted.

It's almost noon.

That might be the mom out on the floor, grinding it with a guy. I tried to talk with her when she came in. But she was kissing this guy. He had his hands on her butt, pulling her tight. Snug.

I collar a few people, not many.

Yup, one says. Died last night. Run down.

Another one tells me the kid was in high school. Played football. Or mebbe basketball.

They're starting a line dance now. I think a couple of these folks are gonna get a room.

I climb back in my car, head down the road. Call my boss.

Tell him I'm gonna skip this one.

Here's an easy way to get a gun...

We got into a real bad patch with folks in Puerto Rico. We'd done some stories about how tons of drugs were getting into Florida. Guess where they were coming from?

Stories about how people had a hard time trying to buy a gun in San Juan. But in Florida, just slightly more difficult than, say, putting on your socks sitting down.

So guys would come to Florida with suitcases of dope, heroin, stashes of cocaine in the soles of their shoes, and trade it for guns. Thriving black market.

When you traced the guns used in crimes on the island, it always led back to Florida.

What was Puerto Rico to do? Well, for one thing, they started offering a whole lot of really rough people immunity from prosecution if they'd snitch on some rougher people. To sweeten the pot, they gave em fake identities, sanitized documents, money.

The bonus? A plane ticket to Orlando. Bottom line was, a bunch of nasties were living in the Sunshine State incognito.

And—oh yeah—nobody in Florida knew anything about it. The whole cop brotherhood thing, kind of a one-way street on this one.

That was the story that really got people in Puerto Rico upset. Bunch of cops, bunch of prosecutors, the governor. All those people denied it. Long and loud.

Consider the fact that, in those days, some of your San Juan neighborhoods were patrolled, not by police, but by the army. Guys with heavy armor... firepower. Two or three folks *a day* getting whacked in San Juan at the time.

The reporters with their arms around all this... Henry Curtis, Jim Leusner, a few others. Coulda found the Lindbergh baby on their lunch hour.

But now there were guys in fancy suits standing in front of microphones calling them liars. And those newspaper stories attracted a lot of attention. So the whole "those reporters are liars" thing got repeated in Tallahassee, at the state capitol, and on the floors of Congress.

That kinda hurt our feelings.

Solution...

Go find the bad guys, the ones who supposedly didn't exist. Those mud-slinging reporters dug in. They started tracking people down.

Who'd they find? Well, there was the woman who ran a drug ring in a little town called Caguas. She was notching maybe 50-grand a week. Minor stuff.

Also very minor... the fact that she happened to be standing by in a parking lot one day when a couple of guys made four people drink gasoline. And then lit a match.

Probably some kind of misunderstanding.

She was comfortably situated in an Orlando suburb. New name, etc.

Also happily relocated:

- a dope-dealing hitman, paid by the wife to whack her tv-star husband;
- a corrupt cop;

- a teenager involved in a mass killing;
- a guy who stood by and watched as a woman got raped and murdered.

Just to name a few.

You calling us liars? Well, explain this...

Now there were more meetings in Tallahassee and in Washington. This time, though, it was Puerto Rico's governor who made the trip.

Called on the carpet. Called north to explain, to apologize.

Yeah.. uh... that stuff in the newspaper. That was true.

Sorry. Won't happen again.

For those slimy, lying reporters... Miller Time.

Chasing a crooked lawyer...

We were collecting string on a big-shot lawyer in town, thought he might be working way outside the lines. And making some serious coin under the table.

Incredibly powerful, uber-connected. He sometimes got defendants off, it seemed, with nothing more than a phone call.

Everybody thought the guy had something going on.

Proving it would be another story.

A mountain of paperwork, boxes full of notes. Checking records at the courthouse, comparing nuggets from cases that had no obvious connection.

But it was beginning to look like there was something there. We'd found a pattern... devious, brilliant, sinister, hugely profitable.

Our work had already taken months.

Then one day an old man showed up at the office. Slouchy hat, trench coat, stuffed briefcase. He was a retired fed. He'd seen something in town that caught his eye, looked shady. He had some time on his hands, so he' done some checking. He was a pro. He knew where to look.

He'd seen us looking in the same places.

Here's a guy who didn't like what he knew. He'd spent a life-time putting guys behind bars. But he was older now, past wanting to do it all himself.

He was going to tell me the story, piece by piece.

And that's where it got bad.

It happened as soon as he got close.

It would be an incredible understatement to say the man had a smell. He had something horrible eating away at his insides. I assumed he was dying. With every breath, he exhaled perhaps the most powerful and abhorrent odor I had ever encountered. It was like an invisible poisonous cloud. He seemed oblivious. But I was leaning to one side, trying not to breathe, backing away as far as I could.

It quickly became more than I could stand.

The man was a gold mine. But I was choking, close to throwing up. Suddenly, my head was splitting. I had started to wonder if he might be infecting me with something. I interrupted, excused myself.

I went to see my boss. Told him very quickly there was a guy outside who knew things we wanted badly. But here was the thing. I was getting as far away from the guy as I could.

My boss could deal with the guy himself, or hand him off to someone else. But I was done. I would not go back. He could accept that, or my immediate resignation.

I walked out the door.

An hour later, I came back. Went to his office. Before I could say a word, he held up a hand.

I thought you were crazy, he said. But that was horrible. I couldn't stand it either.

So?

I told the old fed we'd have to pass.

The story? Never happened. We had a lot, but not all of it. Not enough to prove. Sometimes you have to move on.

About the author

MICHAEL LUDDEN is a former Deputy Managing Editor at the *Orlando Sentinel,* where he directed an investigation that won a Pulitzer Prize. He's written for magazines, advertising and marketing firms, edited books and been a senior writer/editor at CNN's *Headline News.* He lives in Atlanta, where he's working on another Tate Drawdy thriller.

Check out our website at:
www.michaelludden.com

Made in the USA
Columbia, SC
26 April 2018